W9-CTD-709

VOL. 24
Action Edition

Story and Art by
RUMIKO TAKAHASHI

English Adaptation by Gerard Jones

Translation/Mari Morimoto
Touch-Up Art & Lettering/Bill Schuch
Cover and Interior Graphic Design/Yuki Ameda
Editor/Urian Brown

Managing Editor/Annette Roman
Director of Production/Noboru Watanabe
Vice President of Publishing/Alvin Lu
Sr. Director of Acquisitions/Rika Inouye
VP of Sales & Marketing/Liza Coppola
Publisher/Hyoe Narita

Printed in Canada.

Published by VIZ Media, LLC
P.O. Box 77010
San Francisco, CA 94107

Action Edition
10 9 8 7 6 5 4 3 2 1
First printing, December 2005

PARENTAL ADVISORY
INUYASHA is rated T+ for Older Teen. This book contains violence. It is recommended for ages 16 and up.

www.viz.com

store.viz.com

NUYASHA™

VOL. 24 Action Edition

STORY AND ART BY

MIKO TAKAHASHI

CONTENTS

Long ago, in the "Warring States" era of Japan's Muromachi period (*Sengoku-jidai*, approximately 1467-1568 CE), a legendary dog-like half-demon called "Inu-Yasha" attempted to steal the Shikon Jewel—or "Jewel of Four Souls"—from a village, but was stopped by the enchanted arrow of the village priestess, Kikyo. Inu-Yasha fell into a deep sleep, pinned to a tree by Kikyo's arrow, while the mortally wounded Kikyo took the Shikon Jewel with her into the fires of her funeral pyre. Years passed.

Fast-forward to the present day. Kagome, a Japanese high school girl, is pulled into a well one day by a mysterious centipede monster, and finds herself transported into the past—only to come face to face with the trapped Inu-Yasha. She frees him, and Inu-Yasha easily defeats the centipede monster.

The residents of the village, now 50 years older, readily accept Kagome as the reincarnation of their deceased priestess Kikyo, a claim supported by the fact that the Shikon Jewel emerges from a cut on Kagome's body. Unfortunately, the jewel's rediscovery means that the village is soon under attack by a variety of demons in search of this treasure. Then, the jewel is accidentally shattered into many shards, each of which may have the fearsome power of the entire jewel.

Although Inu-Yasha says he hates Kagome because of her resemblance to Kikyo, the woman who "killed" him, he is forced to team up with her when Kaede, the village leader, binds him to Kagome with a powerful spell. Now the two grudging companions must fight to reclaim and reassemble the shattered shards of the Shikon Jewel before they fall into the wrong hands....

THIS VOLUME Miroku's lust for money lands him in trouble again as the reward of a hefty purse provokes him into investigating a mysterious castle cursed by a giant floating ogre head! Then it's time for some monkey business as Inuyasha and pals take on a monkey-god who's gone bananas! And finally the cursed Kohaku

INU-YASHA
Half-demon hybrid, son of a human mother and demon father. His necklace is enchanted, allowing Kagome to control him with a word.

KAGOME
Modern-day Japanese schoolgirl who can travel back and forth between the past and present through an enchanted well.

MIROKU
Lecherous Buddhist priest cursed with a mystical "hellhole" in his hand that's slowly killing him.

NARAKU
Enigmatic demon-mastermind behind the miseries of nearly everyone in the story.

SANGO
"Demon Exterminator" or slayer from the village where the Shikon Jewel was first born.

KOHAKU
Killed by Naraku—but not before first slaying both his own and Sango's father—now he's back again in a newer...if somewhat *slower*...form.

KOGA
Leader of the Wolf Clan, Koga is himself a Wolf Demon and, because of several Shikon shards in his legs, possesses super speed. Enamored of Kagome, he quarrels with Inu-Yasha frequently.

KAGURA
A demon created by Naraku from parts of his body, Kagura—the Wind Demon—is Naraku's second incarnation. Unlike others, however, Kagura resents Naraku's control over her and aids him only for her own survival.

SCROLL ONE

THE OGRE OF THE BURIAL MOUND

WHAT-?! THIS OGRE'S HEAD-

-TOOK THE FULL FORCE OF THE SCAR OF THE WIND?!

WEAPONS WON'T STOP IT!
FSH
MIRO-KU...?
INU-YASHA, WAIT!

HZZ
WE NEED MAGIC!

SHH

IT VAN-ISHED!!
UH...

YES...
PRINCESS... THE OGRE'S HEAD...!

ILLU-SION?
JUST AS I THOUGHT...
...IT WAS ONLY AN ILLUSION.

THEN... THIS THING WILL APPEAR AGAIN TOMORROW?
I EXPECT SO.
FOR ITS ONLY PURPOSE IS TO DIVERT OUR EYES FROM DISCOVERING THE OGRE'S TRUE FORM.
HMPH!

COULD IT BE...
...HE ISN'T JUST HAUNTED BY THE OGRE BUT IS BEING REPLACED BY IT?

...HOO---

SHHHH

SHHH

IF HE SEES US, HE'LL STRIKE...

SWEAK

THEN WE'LL JUST STRIKE BACK, WON'T WE?
EASY. HE'S STILL THIS CASTLE'S LORD, YOU KNOW.

COME ON, MIROKU.
HE'S AN OGRE, ISN'T HE?
I BELIEVE HE'S STILL HUMAN.
BE- SIDES...

THE VAST AURA THAT FILLS THIS CASTLE...
...CAN'T ALL EMANATE FROM THAT ONE SOURCE.

HAIYA!
FSH
BLECH!

SO.
FEEL A LITTLE BETTER NOW, DON'T YA?

SORRY... BUT NO.
KOF
PF PF
...

THAT'S FUNNY.
THIS IS A BLESSED PURIFICATION SALT.
MAKES MOST DEMONS JUST ROLL OVER AND DIE.

TSK. YOU'RE LISTENING TO THIS OLD FRAUD?
MAY AS WELL USE SAND.
TM TM
WEL-COME BACK.
PEH PEH

MY FATHER...
MAY BE AN OGRE...?

THEN...
BUT THE MONK DISAGREES. HE BELIEVES OUR LORD IS MERELY POSSESSED...

...AND THAT THE TRUE OGRE LURKS ELSEWHERE.
OH MY...
LORD MONK?
YES?
THE PRINCESS WISHES TO DISCUSS SOME MATTERS WITH YOU.
DOES SHE?
PWIK

HEY.
YOU DON'T THINK YOU'RE GOING ALONE, DO YOU?

FEAR NOT, SANGO.
FOR AS BEAUTIFUL AS THE PRINCESS IS...
GRIP

MY HEART BELONGS TO YOU.
DO YOU THINK I GIVE A DAMN?
RUB RUB

WE DON'T KNOW WHEN THE OGRE'S GOING TO COME BACK!
SO IT'S DANGEROUS TO SPLIT UP-REMEMBER?!

IF THAT'S WHAT YOU'RE WORRYING ABOUT, DON'T.
MIROKU CAN TAKE CARE OF HIMSELF IN A FIGHT.

GLARE
YOU ARE SUCH AN IDIOT.
GEEZ! WHO'S THE OGRE HERE?!
DUCK

LORD MONK.
MM?

YES, OF COURSE. THANK YOU.
UH...
TAKE A PINCH O' THE PURIFICATION SALT.
JUST IN CASE...
THE OGRE'S HEAD BURIAL MOUND...
IT HAS BEEN ENSHRINED.
YES... IN THE CELLAR OF THIS CASTLE...
HOOOO...
AND THERE HAD NOT BEEN A SINGLE STRANGE OCCURRENCE... UNTIL NOW.
YES.
I HEARD THAT THE OGRE'S HEAD HAD BEEN BURIED TO AVERT OCCULT MISCHIEF, BUT...
I VERY MUCH WANT YOU TO SEE IT, LORD MONK.

HYOOO

BUT THEN THE MOUND WAS VIOLATED...

AND THE OGRE ESCAPED.

WHO...?

INU-YASHA SIT!

WHAT DO YOU EXPECT, LEAVING HIM ALONE WITH THAT PRINCESS?
PWIK

THAT MONK'S SURE TAKING HIS TIME.

...WE SHOULD GO CHECK ON HIM?
BUT SANGO... MAYBE...

JUST WHEN I THINK YOU CAN'T GET ANY DUMBER!
WHAT IS THIS?!
WOOSH

SHE'S TRYING TOO HARD...
I DON'T NEED TO EMBARRASS MYSELF.
HE'S A BIG BOY.

!
YAAAA!
TOOM...

GUH GUH GUH...

KCHI KCHI KCHI

RRIP
RRIP

HOOO...

THESE...
...ARE THE REMAINS OF THE MONKS AND PRIESTESSES WHO CAME TO EXORCISE THE OGRE.

FOR WHEN THE OGRE LIVED...
...IT WAS SAID TO HAVE A TASTE FOR THOSE WITH MYSTIC POWERS. IT ADDED THEIR POWERS TO ITS OWN.

IS THIS WHY YOU BROUGHT ME HERE...?

YES.
I WANT YOUR POWERS, DEAR MONK.

ZHOO
I PUT A SPELL ON THE EXORCIST'S SALT.
IT SEEMS TO HAVE GIVEN IT SOME EFFECT.
SSS...
NGH...

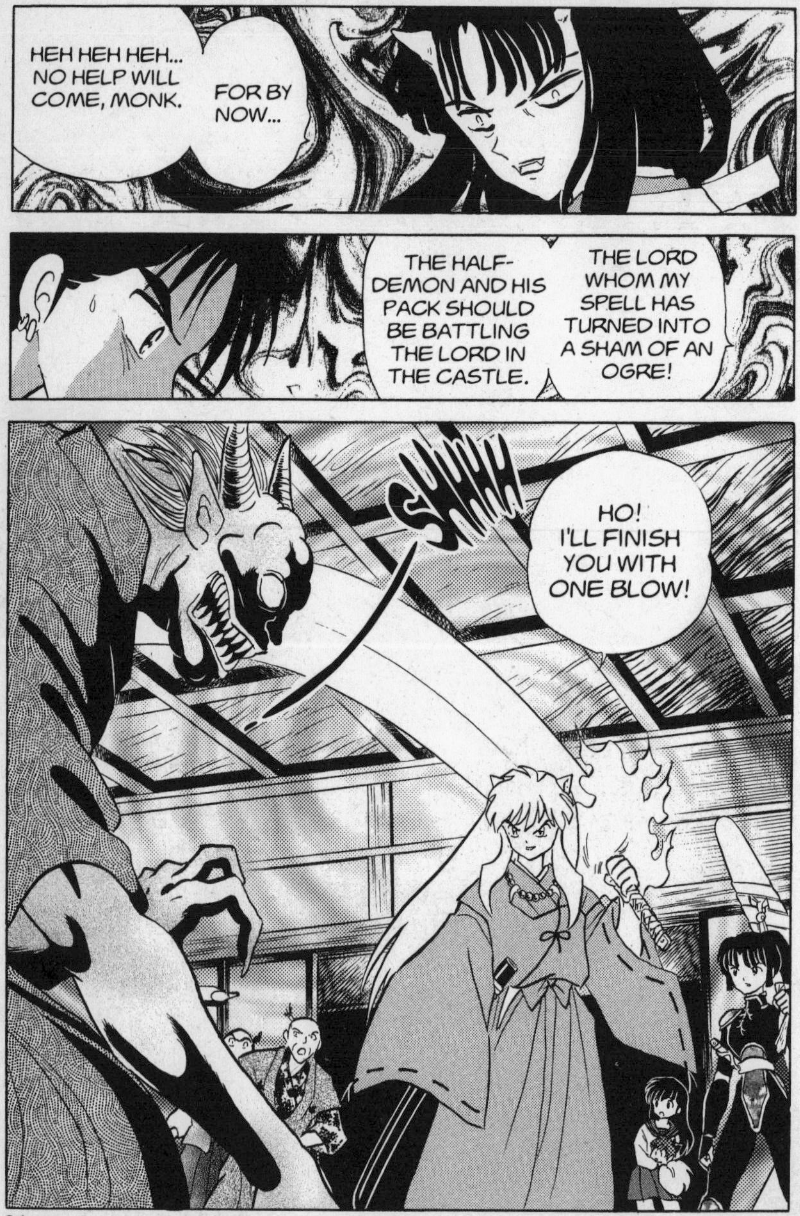

THE HALF-DEMON AND HIS PACK SHOULD BE BATTLING THE LORD IN THE CASTLE.

THE LORD WHOM MY SPELL HAS TURNED INTO A SHAM OF AN OGRE!

SHHHH

HO! I'LL FINISH YOU WITH ONE BLOW!

SCROLL TWO
THE PRINCESS VESSEL

PRETTY BRASSY OF YOU JUST TO SAUNTER IN LIKE THIS, OGRE.

M-MY LORD...

WHIP
YEEE!
!

INU-YASHA! DON'T USE TETSUSAIGA!
IT'S USING HER AS A SHIELD-!

ZZK
SSSSHH
CLAWS OF STEEL!!

SWOOK
!
OH, NO YOU DON'T!
VSH
SHHHH
TM

SHUNK
DM

H-HE'S GONE...
WHEW
FOOL! IT'S STILL TOO EARLY TO RELAX!

YOU WOMEN PROTECT THE PRINCESS!
BUT...
SHE...

THE OGRE'S HEAD BURIAL MOUND IN THE CELLAR?!

Y-YES, MA'AM.
SHE SAID SHE WANTED THE MONK TO SEE IT...

SANGO!
TM
WE'VE GOT TO GET MIROKU!

I'M COMIN' TOO.
IT'S SAFER THAN HERE.
ARE YOU SURE YOU'RE AN EXOR-CIST?
TROT TROT

WHY DON'T YOU SMILE? THIS IS GOOD NEWS!
WHAT?

C'MON, I KNOW YOU WERE SCARED!
YOU THOUGHT THE MONK AND THE PRINCESS WERE GETTIN' TOO FRIENDLY, EH?

BUT IF THEY'RE AT THAT BURIAL MOUND-
IT'S PROBABLY NOTHING TO WORRY 'BOUT! UNLESS THEY'RE REALLY KINKY...
AGH!!
DON'T MAKE ME SICK!

HEH HEH HEH... YOU CANNOT MOVE, CAN YOU, MONK?
NO ONE CAN SLIP THROUGH THE PARALYZING POWER OF MY AURA...
HOOOOO...

YOU... PLAN TO DEVOUR ME...?

HEH... OF ALL THE EXORCISING MONKS AND PRIESTESSES I HAVE DEVOURED...

...YOU, MONK, WILL BE THE 100TH.

WHEN I SWALLOW YOU, PRIESTLY POWERS AND ALL...
...I SHALL BE COMPLETELY RESTORED.
THEN I SHALL BID FARE-WELL TO THIS PATHETIC FORM.

HIS WOUNDS ARE SHALLOW.
WE'VE GOT TO STOP THE BLEED-ING.

THERE MIGHT BE SOMEONE STILL ALIVE!
LET'S GO!
THE OGRE... GOT THEM ALL.
OH.

THE BEDROOM WHERE THE LORD CONFINED HIMSELF...
THIS ROOM...
IS ANYONE HERE...?

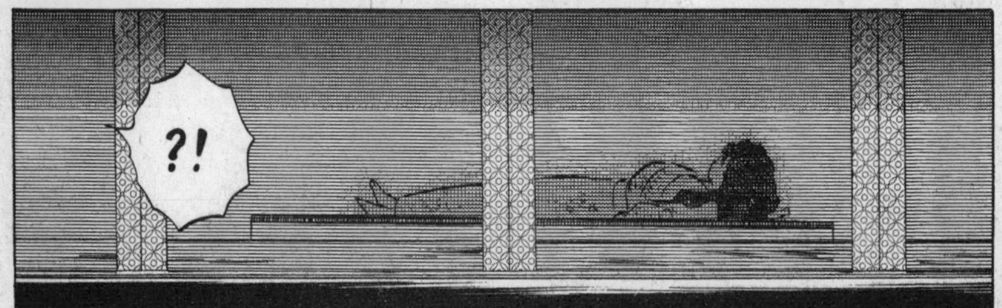
?!

SOMEONE'S...
SLEEPING...?

UM~

WHAT...?!
THE
PRINCESS...?!

!
TWIK

WENT TO THE BURIAL MOUND IN THE CELLAR...?

BUT... I THOUGHT THE PRINCESS...

SHE'S DEAD?!
VSH

VWW
FEH.
RUNNING AROUND ALL OVER.

?!

SOMETHING'S FISHY ABOUT THIS OGRE...

HE JUST KEEPS RUNNING AND DOESN'T COME AT ME AT ALL...

AS IF...

HE'S BUYING TIME...

HOOOO...

!

TM

!

MONK!

NOW YOU WILL WATCH...

...AS I DEVOUR THE MONK.

KRIII

NO...

I...CAN'T LET HER...

!
PFF
TRY THIS!
PURIFI-CATION SALT!

DUMP ALL YOUR SALT ON HER!
MADAME EXORCIST!

WHY ISN'T SHE PARALYZED?!
THIS HAG...

HUH...?!

LIKE THIS?

RRG!
KRAK

AUGH!

BZZT BZZT

I'M IMPRESSED, MADAME EXORCIST.
I THOUGHT NOTHING COULD NULLIFY THAT OGRE'S EVIL AURA.

I THOUGHT I WAS GOING TO DIE...
ARE YOU ALL RIGHT?!
FUMP

L... LORD MONK...
WOBBLE

IN A WAY, THIS MAKES IT MORE AMAZING...
SHE REALLY DOESN'T FEEL IT...
ULP
EVIL AURA...?
THERE WAS AN EVIL AURA?

SHHHH...
!

IT FLEW OFF AND ESCAPED ON ITS OWN!

THAT OGRE'S HEAD-
WELL, THIS IS NO TIME TO BE SITTIN' ON YOUR HAUNCHES!

IT'S GROWING?!
THE AURA-!

!

SCROLL THREE
A GREATER AURA

HOOO!!
THE AURA'S RISING UP FROM INSIDE THE CASTLE!

YOU JUST GET BACK INSIDE THERE!
WHOK
BIK BIK

THE... OGRE'S HEAD?

HSSSS...

GRR...

SSSS...

FROM INSIDE THE PRINCESS' BODY...?!

GLP GLP

WH... WHAT'S IT EATING?!

JUST ONE MORE...
BUT I DIDN'T GET TO DEVOUR THE MONK.
HEH...I HAVE THE POWERS OF 99 DEAD PRIESTS STORED IN THE PRINCESS' DEAD BODY.
WHAT DO YOU HAVE INSIDE YOUR BOSOM...?
YOUNG MAID...
THE SHIKON SHARDS...
HEH HEH HEH...
THIS, I THINK, WILL WORK EVEN BETTER THAN THE PRIESTLY POWERS OF A MERE HUMAN...
B-BMP

IT WANTS TO EAT THEM?!
VISH

ZZZ
!

KRUNCH!
AIEE!

OH-HO!!

IT'S... THE OGRE...
IS IT UNCONSCIOUS?!
SSSSSS

THEY WERE SO DESPERATE TO BE FREE OF OCCULT MISCHIEF THAT THEY BURIED MY HEAD IN THE GROUND.

...THE POOR FOOLS.

THAT'S WHY I KILLED THEIR LITTLE PRINCESS AND STOLE HER FORM.
AND WHY I USED HER CORPSE AS A VESSEL FOR THE POWERS I STOLE FROM ALL THOSE EXORCISTS.

SO THE LORD WAS JUST A WATCHDOG FOR THE PRINCESS' CORPSE-
AND YOUR DECOY WHENEVER YOU WERE ABOUT TO BE FOUND OUT!

WELL THEN, IT'S TOO BAD, HEAD-
THAT WE HAD TO FIND YOU OUT!
HEH HEH HEH...

THE MONK...
WHY HAVE YOU NOT COME OUT OF THE BURIAL MOUND BEFORE THIS?
T-M

AN OGRE WITH AS MUCH POWER AS YOU SHOULD HAVE BEEN ABLE TO COME OUT WHENEVER YOU WANTED.

YOU'RE SO POWERFUL THAT YOU GAVE EVEN ME TROUBLE.

BECAUSE I KNEW THAT I'D HAVE BEEN ABSORBED BY AN EVEN GREATER EVIL AURA... AND TAKEN OVER BY IT.
BECAUSE... IF I'D VENTURED OUT TOO SOON, IT WOULD HAVE BEEN THE END OF ME.

?!

OR RATH-ER...

A CONGLOM-ERATION OF AURAS... CALLED NARAKU.

BUT NARAKU IS NO LONGER IN THIS LAND...

SO I NEED NOT HIDE MYSELF ANY LONGER!

I'M AFRAID NOT!!

HE DID IT...
HOOOO...
SHHHH...
!
!
RRRIP

THE SCAR OF THE WIND ISN'T ENOUGH ...
IT'S STILL ALIVE!
DAMN.

I'LL TAKE ANOTHER BODY AND RAVAGE THIS LAND AGAIN!
HEH HEH HEH...THIS IS JUST THE BEGINNING.
SHEE...

HOO
?!
TUG

WIND TUNNEL!

SO THAT'S WHY ALL THE DEMONS AROUND HERE HAVE BEEN RAMPAGING?
BECAUSE THIS "NARAKU" HAS GONE MISSIN'?
SO IT SEEMS...
THAT MEANS I'LL BE GETTIN' BUSIER AND BUSIER!
THIS IS GONNA BE A GREAT SEASON!
EH?
NOTHING PERSONAL, CRONE... BUT IT'S TIME TO RETIRE.
YOU'RE JUST A FAKE ANYWAY, RIGHT?
YOU COULD BE A LITTLE MORE DIPLO-MATIC...
FAKE, AM I?
AND IF I HADN'T BEEN THERE, YOUR MONK FRIEND WOULD BE INSIDE THAT OGRE!
YOU'VE GIVEN HER CONFI-DENCE.
I DON'T THINK SHE NEEDS ANYONE TO GIVE HER CONFIDENCE...

THIS IS QUITE BOTHER-SOME, ISN'T IT?

THANKS TO NARAKU'S ABSENCE, EVEN THE DEMONS THAT HAVE BEEN IN HIDING ARE STARTING TO CAUSE TROUBLE.

NAH.

THEY'RE ALL PIPSQUEAK DEMONS WHO WERE LYING LOW IN FEAR OF NARAKU ANYWAY.

WE CAN JUST TAKE THEM DOWN ONE AFTER ANOTHER.

SCROLL FOUR
THE VENERABLE MONKEY GOD

THIS PLACE SURE LOOKS PEACEFUL.

I DON'T IMAGINE WE'LL FIND ANY CLUES TO NARAKU HERE.

VILLAGERS...?
MMM-?
HUH...?

IT'S THE SILVER-HAIRED ONE!
IT'S TRUE! THOSE EARS! HE'S NOT HUMAN!

WHAT DO YOU PEOPLE WANT?
HSS
THEY'RE TALKING ABOUT YOU, INU-YASHA!

UH?
O VENERABLE DOG GOD! PLEASE HELP US...
BOW

DOG... GOD...?
YOU MEAN ME?

NO ONE CAN HELP US NOW BUT THE GODS... PLEASE!
YOU ARE IN TROU-BLE...?
OUR FIELDS HAVE BEEN RAIDED ONCE AGAIN!
UNLESS WE ARE SAVED, WE WILL STARVE TO DEATH...

WAS THIS A DEMON'S DOING...?
NOPE, NOT A DE-MON...
MONKEYS.
MONKEYS...

THE OLD TALES SAY THAT MONKEYS FEAR DOGS.
PLEASE DEFEND US, O VENERABLE DOG GOD!

OF COURSE.
WE SHALL GET RID OF THEM.
HEY, HEY!
WE DON'T HAVE TIME FOR THIS!
RE-LAX.
SANGO AND I WILL GO SEARCHING FOR CLUES TO NARAKU IN THE MEANTIME.
THAT'S RIGHT.

WE CALL THIS "MONKEY FOREST"... FOR HERE OUR TORMENTORS HIDE.
BUT WE KNOW YOU CAN DRIVE THEM OUT, O VENERABLE-

ENOUGH, ALREADY.
MUTTER MUTTER
HOW DID I GET STUCK WITH MONKEY DUTY?

KSSH

EH?!

DIE, DOG!

YEEEE!

THIS HAS **GOT** TO BE A DEMON!

GUH.

PSHWOO

POP

ARE YOU THE ONES WHO RAIDED THOSE FIELDS?
HEY.
THEY'RE SO CUTE!
BABY MON-KEYS!
HUH?!

PSS PSS
PSS PSS
PSS PSS

...IS A COMMON TRICK OF US MINOR DEMONS. I WAS GOING TO SAY, DON'T TAKE IT. BUT...

...TOO LATE.

RM

BETCHA CAN'T MOVE, DOG DEMON!
WA HA HA HA HA HA!

WHOOSH
TALK FASTER NEXT TIME!

NOW! NO MORE STUPID PRANKS, OR-

BONK
BANG
BANG

HO HO! THREATEN-ING US IS USELESS!
UNTIL WE UNDO THE SPELL, THAT BOULDER WILL NEVER PART FROM YOUR HAND!

WELL... IN THAT CASE...
HSSS

BOOOM

I'LL JUST HAVE TO HIT YOU WITH ***THIS*** HAND!

BRR BRR BRR

YEEP!

WE'VE GOTTA CATCH 'EM!
VSH
LET'S GO, SHIPPO!

KAGOME! HEY!
DOMM
YOU WAIT THERE, INU-YASHA!
IT'LL BE BAD IF WE DON'T CATCH 'EM!
HUH?

JUST LIKE THEY SAID-
ILLUSION SPELLS CAN ONLY BE UNDONE BY THE ONE WHO CAST THEM!
OH MY.
TM
TM

TMTM

SHK...

A TINY SHRINE...

IT'S NOT MISCHIEF.
WHY DO MISCHIEF TO THE VILLAGE'S FIELDS?
VIP

WE'RE SEARCHING FOR OUR KIDNAPPED VENERABLE MONKEY GOD.

HE IS SUPPOSED TO RESIDE IN THIS SHRINE.

VENERABLE... MONKEY GOD...

WERE IN TRAINING TO GUARD THIS HOLY SITE.
WE SPRITES WHO SERVE THE VENERABLE ONE...

AND THE HOLY OBJECT, IN WHICH THE VENERABLE MONKEY GOD RESIDES, WAS CARRIED OFF BY VILLAINS UNKNOWN!
BUT DURING A WAR, THE SHRINE BURNED TO THE GROUND...

YUP.
SO YOU'RE SAYING THE MONKEY GOD'S HOLY OBJECT IS SOMEWHERE IN THAT VILLAGE?

ME TOO, ME TOO!
I HAD A DREAM TOO!
...HAVE RECEIVED DIVINE DREAM MESSAGES FROM OUR GOD!
FOR I...
WE KNOW THAT THE HOLY OBJECT IS BURIED SOMEWHERE IN THE VILLAGE FIELDS.

HE TOLD ME IT SMELLS LIKE VEGETABLES AND HE DOESN'T LIKE IT.
HE TOLD ME HE IS IN A TIGHT, NARROW SPACE.
HE TOLD ME HE IS IN A DARK, DANK PLACE.

...BOO—OOM
M?

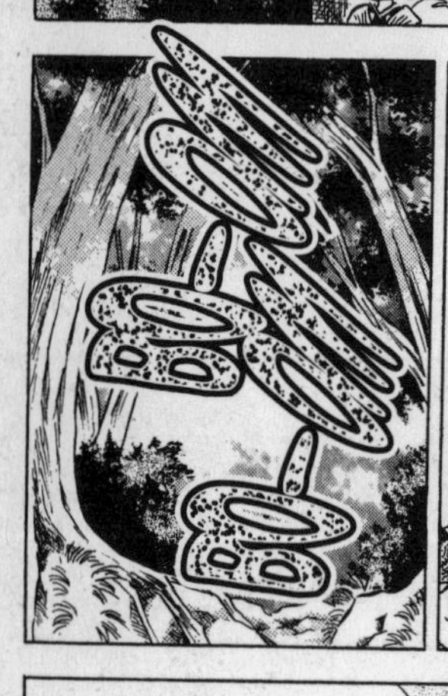
BOOM

BOOM
SOMETHING'S... APPROACHING.

YOU KNOW...

YOU MIGHT WANT TO UNDO THAT SPELL YOU CAST ON INU-YASHA...AND FAST.
WE CAN'T.

FOR...
DUHHH
...WE FORGOT HOW TO UNDO IT!

YOU'D BETTER BE JOKING!
PANT PANT
YEEK!

DIE.
...HOOP
WAIT!

WE LEARNED THIS SPELL FROM OUR VENERABLE MONKEY GOD.

IF WE CAN FIND THE HOLY OBJECT, HE WILL TEACH US TO UNDO IT!

THEN WE'VE GOT TO FIND THAT OBJECT IN A HURRY.
LET'S GO, INU-YASHA!
WRRL
UH...

I'M GONNA GO AHEAD, OK?
YOU SHOULD'VE JUST STAYED PUT.
AREN'T YOU TIRED, INU-YASHA?
DON'T ASK.
DRAG DRAG

SCROLL FIVE
THE HOLY OBJECT

WE KNOW IT'S HERE!

GIVE IT BACK!

BUT WE DON'T KNOW ANYTHING ABOUT IT.

BOOM

GAH!

HE'S HERE AL-READY!

BO—OM
HUH?
OUR LIVES DEPEND ON THIS, YOU KNOW!
HEY, WHAT ARE YOU ALL STANDING AROUND FOR?

V... VENER-ABLE DOG GOD?
DUCK

DOOOOM
PANT PANT PANT

WHAT ABOUT THIS MONKEY GOD?!

ACK! DON'T GET ANY CLOSER TO HIM!
THAT WAS QUICK, INU-YASHA.
GRRR
IF WE DON'T GET THIS ROCK OFF, SOMEBODY'S GONNA PAY!
TP TP

YOUR HAND IS STUCK TO A STONE BECAUSE OF THE MONKEYS' SPELL...?
MUTTER

ARE YOU SURE YOU'RE THE DOG GOD?
DID I EVER CLAIM TO BE YOUR STUPID DOG GOD?!
I'D SAY YOU'RE ABOUT THE FARTHEST THING FROM IT.

THEY SAY THAT ONLY THE VENERABLE MONKEY GOD KNOWS HOW TO UNDO THE SPELL.
DO YOU GET IT NOW?

IF YOU'RE HOLDING OUT ON US FOR ANY REASON...
I'LL LEVEL THIS VILLAGE!

JUST HUSH AND WAIT PATIENTLY.
KAGOME... YOU...

INU-YASHA, SIT!

I'M REALLY, REALLY SORRY.
BOW BOW
IT WOULD BE A SHAME TO HAVE HIM GO ON A RAMPAGE.
SHUFFLE SHUFFLE
I SUPPOSE WE SHOULD SPLIT UP AND SEARCH FOR IT.

INU-YASHA...
WE'RE BAAACK!

CAW CAW

THE VILLAGERS DON'T SEEM TO KNOW A THING ABOUT THIS "HOLY OBJECT."
BUT FROM THE LOOKS OF IT...

WHAT ARE YOU DOING?
KICK KICK
YOU DIDN'T SEE ANYTHING- GOT IT?!

WE CHECKED UNDER FLOORBOARDS ... DREDGED THE IRRIGATION PONDS... BUT...
THERE IS NO HINT OF A HOLY OBJECT.

EVERYONE'S BEEN AWFULLY BUSY WHILE WE WERE GONE...
IT IS A PROB- LEM.
I UNDER- STAND.
I'LL TRY TO DO SOME- THING WITH MY PRIESTLY POWERS.
EH?
YOU'RE GOING TO TRY TO FIND OUR GOD?!

I JUST THOUGHT IT WOULD BE NICE TO HAVE A NIGHT'S LODGING.
WHY IS THAT?
PSS

THAT'S FINE!
I CANNOT USE MY POWERS UNTIL THE MORNING.

OF COURSE. BUT...

THERE'S SOMETHING ODD ABOUT THIS...
PSS PSS
ACTUALLY, YOU'RE STUPID.
WE'RE SAVED!
THEY'LL PROBABLY FIND THE THING BY THEN.
PSS PSS
THAT IS SO SLEAZY... EVEN FOR YOU.

OOOOMMM
SIGH.

YOU DON'T HAVE TO KEEP ME COMPANY.
KAGOME, YOU GO INSIDE TOO.

AND WHY WOULD I BE LONELY?!
BUT WON'T YOU BE LONELY OUT HERE BY YOURSELF?

GEEZ.
REALLY?
YOU'RE NOT BOTHERING ME!
ARGH!
WELL, IF I'M REALLY BOTHER-ING YOU...

AREN'T THERE ANY OTHER CLUES...?
THIS IS ALL SO WEIRD...

GLEEM
HUH?

OH...
UM... WHAT'S THIS...?

WE DON'T HAVE MUCH TO OFFER GUESTS BUT PICKLED VEGETABLES.
WE'RE A POOR VILLAGE.

WAIT!
THAT'S QUITE A GLOW.
IS SOME-THING WRONG WITH THEM?

THESE VEGETABLES WERE HARVESTED FROM YOUR FIELDS, YES?
THIS IS THE VENERABLE MONKEY GOD'S UNMISTAK-ABLE GLOW!

JUST AS THE DIVINE DREAMS STATED...
DARK AND DANK...
TIGHT AND NARROW...
AND SMELLING LIKE VEGETABLES!

THEN HE'S IN THE FIELDS AFTER ALL?!
B—OOM

HE MUST BE BURIED DEEP UNDER-GROUND.
THEN LET'S DIG UP THIS VILLAGE FROM END TO END!

WAH! IT'S THE HOLY OBJECT!

THIS STONE YOU USE FOR PICKLING...

...IS GLOWING.

WE DON'T SEE ANYTHING...

GLOWING...?

YAKYAK

...GLEEEEEM

THIS IS... THIS IS SACRILEGE!
AND YOU HAD IT HIDDEN HERE ALL ALONG!
BUT WE PICKED THAT UP JUST OUTSIDE THE VILLAGE.
IT WAS THE PERFECT SIZE FOR A PICKLING STONE...

YOU MEAN RIGHT OUTSIDE MONKEY FOREST...?
LIAR! THE HOLY OBJECT WAS IN THE SHRINE DEEP INSIDE THE FOREST!
BUT IT'S TRUE.
WE WERE GUARDING IT WITH OUR LIVES!
THAT'S RIGHT! EVEN...

...WHEN THE SHRINE WAS BURNING FROM THE BATTLE, WE RESCUED IT AND...

IT SHOULD BE SAFE WAY OVER HERE!
HF HF HF HF

OO! ACORNS!

LOTS OF ACORNS!
HERE TOO!
AND OVER HERE!
GLOP GLOP
GLOP GLOP

AHA!
POMP

...IN OTHER WORDS, YOU FORGOT IT THERE.

I HAVE BEEN WAITING FOR YOOOO—
DA—DUM
VENER-ABLE MONKEY GOD!

I STILL SMELL LIKE VEGETA-BLES.
WAAA! WE MISSED YOU SO MUCH!

I HOPE YOU HAVEN'T BEEN MISCHIEVOUS WHILE I WAS GONE.
OH NO, NOT AT ALL...
HEY!
BOOOM
MEMORY TROUBLES...

CHI CHI

THE VENERABLE MONKEY GOD PROMISES...
THAT IF YOU ERECT A NEW SHRINE FOR HIM, HE WILL PROTECT YOUR VILLAGE.
IT SHALL BE DONE.

AREN'T YOU GLAD, INU-YASHA? GETTING THAT ROCK OFF YOUR HAND?
PEH. WHAT A WASTE OF A TRIP THAT WAS!

DEAR, BRILLIANT GIRL. FOR BEING ABLE TO PINPOINT MY WHEREABOUTS, ACCEPT MY THANKS... ...AND MY PRAISE.
OH, NO...
IT WAS PRETTY EASY, REALLY.

YOU WERE ALL JUST TOO STUPID.
WHO ARE YOU TO TALK? YOU'RE THE ONE WHO WANTED TO DIG UP THE FIELDS!

I AM GLAD THAT I WAS NOT TRAPPED THERE ANY LONGER. THE ODDITIES OUTSIDE CON-CERNED ME.
ODDI-TIES...?

SOON AFTER I ENTERED THAT PICKLING JAR...

A VAST EVIL AURA, THE LIKES OF WHICH I HAVE NEVER FELT BEFORE...

PASSED THROUGH THE SKY ABOVE THIS VILLAGE.

WHERE DID THAT AURA GO?!
AND?

IT SIMPLY... VAN-ISHED.
IT DID NOT FADE INTO THE DIS-TANCE.

VANISHED?!

IT VANISHED.

NO MISTAKE. IT'S NARAKU.
INU-YASHA...

SHALL WE GO?

YEAH.

AT LEAST NOW WE HAVE A DIRECTION TO GO!

SCROLL SIX

THE GHOST

TMTM
HHHHHH

ZSH
ZSSH
!

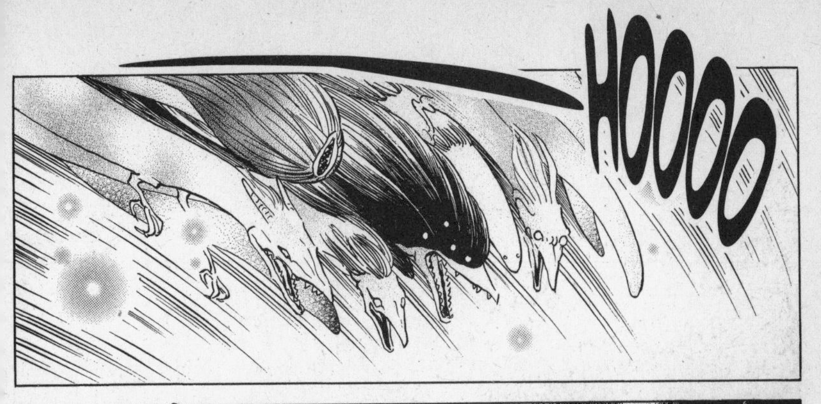
HOOOO

WKK
WKK
SHHHH

VSSH

WRKK
WRKK

ENOUGH!
RRAK
RRAK

I HAD ABANDONED MY TERR-ITORY...

...AND FLED FROM THE NORTH.

THOSE OTHERS... DID THE SAME...

FLED...

FROM WHAT?

HE CAME DOWN FROM EVEN FURTHER NORTH...
...THAN MY TERRITORY.
HE IS NEITHER DEMON... NOR HUMAN.
FROM HIS BODY CAME THE SCENT OF DEATH...AND HUMAN GRAVES.
HE BEGAN...
...DE-VOURING... ALL THE DEMONS IN THE AREA...

HSS...

WHAT ARE WE GOING TO DO, KOGA?

I THOUGHT WE WERE SEARCHING FOR NARAKU.
YOU MEAN... TO WHERE THAT GHOST IS?
LET'S GO.

...YOU MEAN INU-YASHA?

BESIDES WHICH...
...THAT INSOLENT PUPPY'S HEADED THIS WAY.

THAT'S WHY WE'RE GOING TO CHECK IT OUT.
YOU DON'T THINK THEY'RE RELATED?

IT STINKS OF WOLVES!

WOLVES...?

WHAT KIND OF SCENT IS THAT?
THAT DAMNED KOGA! I CAN SMELL HIS CONCEIT!
NOT JUST ANY WOLVES-

I WONDER IF HE STUMBLED ONTO A CLUE.
THEN KOGA TOO IS HEADING TOWARD THE OX-TIGER, EH?

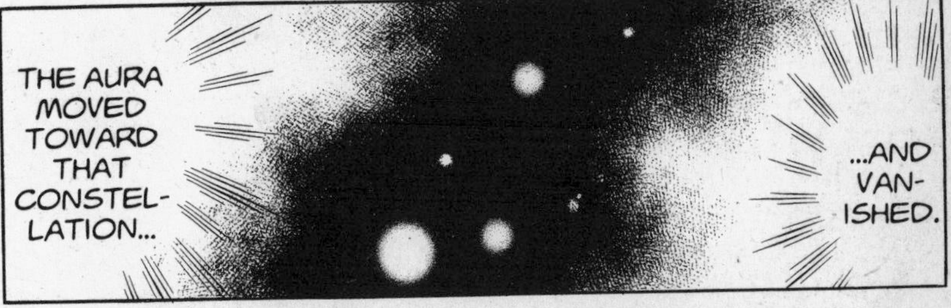
THE AURA MOVED TOWARD THAT CONSTEL-LATION...
...AND VAN-ISHED.

WE'RE GOING TO SPEED IT UP!
HSH
SOMEWHERE OUT THERE... IS NARAKU.

HMPH. HOW COWARDLY.
SKH SHK
WOULDN'T IT BE BETTER IF WE TURNED BACK TO THE VILLAGE AND SOUGHT SHELTER...?
FATHER... THE SUN IS GOING DOWN.

HEH. IF THERE IS SUCH A THING...
RUMORS HAVE IT THAT A GIANT OGRE HAS BEEN SIGHTED IN THESE PARTS RECENTLY.

VSSH

I SHALL DISPEL IT WITH MY PRIESTLY POWERS!

CHOMK CHOMK

CHOMK

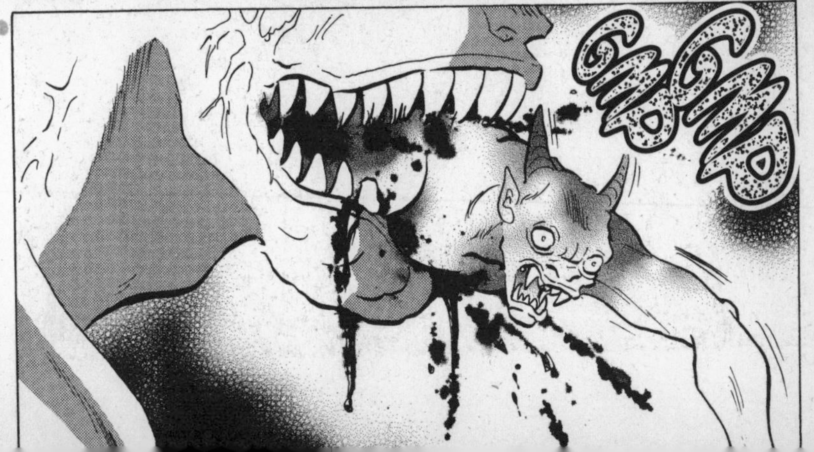

WHAT...?
AN OGRE... DEVOURING ANOTHER OGRE...?

HSSSSS

F-FATHER... YOUR PRIESTLY POWERS...
UH...

NOT RIGHT NOW!
ZZZZZOOM

LORD KYOKO-TSU.

HMM?

ONE WHO POSSESSES SHIKON SHARDS.
HE APPROACHES THE VICINITY...

YOU CAN GO NOW.
KOHAKU... OR SO YOU SAID YOUR NAME WAS.

SO IT WAS WORTH IT FOR ME TO HAVE COME OUT HERE BEFORE MY ELDER BROTHERS, AFTER ALL.
HEH HEH HEH... I SEE...

GLEEEM

AT LEAST... THAT'S WHAT I WISH I COULD SAY. BUT...

LET ME TAKE THE SHARD IN YOUR BACK TOO WHILE I'M AT IT!

SPHUU

DO NOT EXCEED YOUR LIMITS.
BZZ...

TMP

HEH HEH HEH... SO I'M BEING WATCHED, EH?
ZZZ...

I PRIZE MY LIFE TOO.
SIGH... ALL RIGHT.
VP

BLICH

HEH HEH HEH HEH...
GLEEM
AFTER ALL, I DID JUST REGAIN IT...

D-DM D-DM

HSSH
DMM
KRAKAKAK

I'M GONNA TAKE THEM...

...AND YOUR LIFE, TOO.

WOO...!

EEEEE...!

SCROLL SEVEN
KYOKOTSU

IT'S JUST LIKE THAT OLD WOLF SAID.

I CAN SMELL IT...

IT'S BEEN QUITE A WHILE SINCE I EMERGED FROM THE GRAVE.
HEH HEH HEH... I STILL STINK, EH?

YOU'RE A LIVELY ONE...

I'VE GOT TO EAT MORE...GET SOME MORE FRESH BLOOD AND FLESH INTO ME.

THEN HE IS A GHOST?
HE'S NOT DENYING IT.

COME BE LORD KYOKOTSU'S FLESH AND BLOOD!

WE STILL HAVE SOME TALKING TO DO!

KARARA
GM GMGMGM

THEY'RE IN YOUR LEGS, EH?
I SEE.
KARA..
HSH..
TP
GLEEM

SHIKON SHARDS IN YOUR LEGS...
KARA-

JUST WHAT ARE YOU?
YOU SAID YOUR NAME WAS KYOKO-TSU?

HE'S NOT ONE OF THAT DEMON'S SPAWN...
I DON'T SMELL NARAKU'S SCENT COMING FROM HIM.

I'M A MAN, OF COURSE.
WHAT AM I?
GCHE GCHE

HE CAN'T BE!
PSS PSS
A HUMAN...?

WOULD COME BACK TO LIFE FROM THE GRAVE?
HMPH... YOU'RE SAYING A MERE MAN...

HEH HEH HEH.
THANKS TO THIS SHIKON SHARD...
I FEEL EVEN BETTER NOW THAN WHEN I WAS ALIVE!

A SHIKON SHARD!
HOW DID YOU GET A HOLD OF THAT?!

WHAT WILL THAT MATTER-
WHEN YOU'RE IN MY GUT!!

DO YOU REALLY THINK YOU CAN CATCH ME WITH SUCH SLOW MOVEMENTS?
HEH.
BAM
CRACK
CRRK
!
VSH
SLAP

OHH...
K-KOGA!

GRAB
WHO ARE YOU TRYING TO HIT-

VNN
-IDIOT?!

KLATTER
DOOOM

H-HE DID IT!
YES!

FEH... HOW DISAP-POINTING...
TAK
TAK

!
TWIK-!!

GAAH!
KSSSH

GRAB
UGH!
KOGA-!!

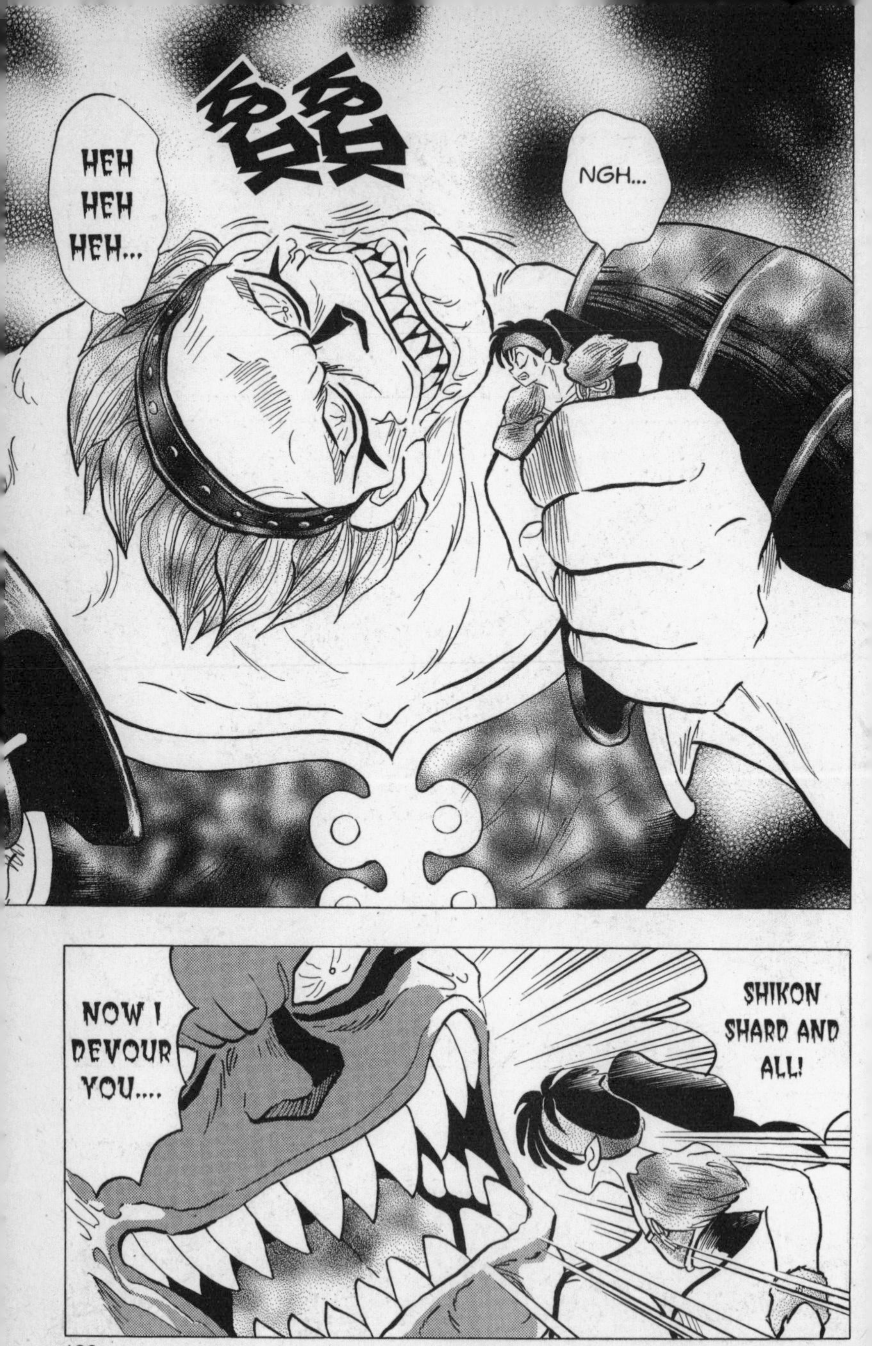

NGH...

HEH HEH HEH...

ENOUGH OF THIS!

IT DOESN'T EVEN ITCH...
HEH HEH HEH...

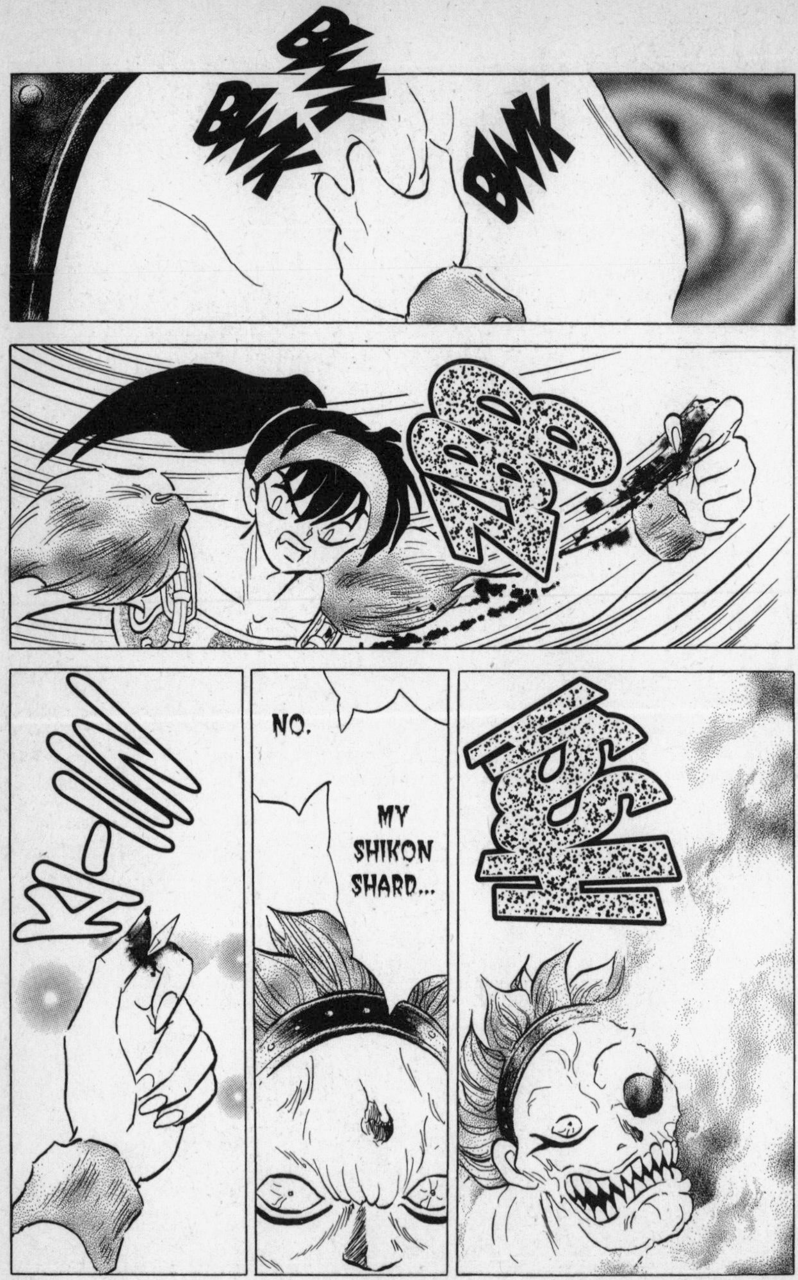

NO.

MY SHIKON SHARD...

KOGA!
NGH...
GLEEM
!
BZZ...

KITTIN

THOSE...
ARE NARAKU'S POISON INSECTS...

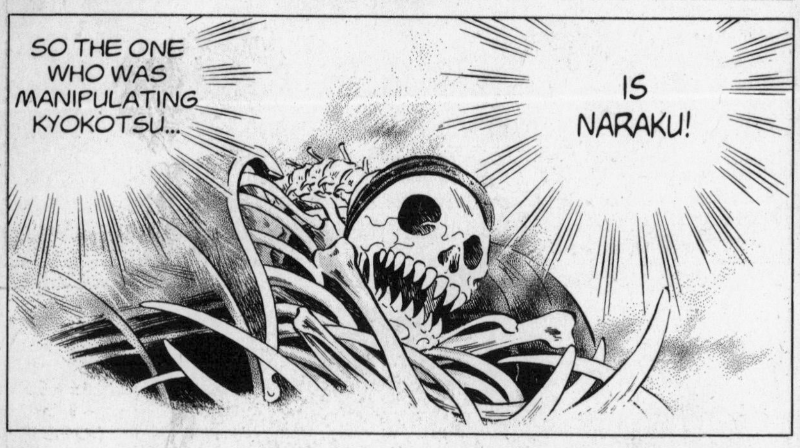
SO THE ONE WHO WAS MANIPULATING KYOKOTSU...
IS NARAKU!

SO DID KYOKOTSU DIE?
HUH.

YES, LORD JYAKOTSU.
HE WAS A FOOL IN THE END.

WELL, I GUESS IT CAN'T BE HELPED.
HE WAS THE WEAKEST ONE AMONG US.

SO, WHAT NOW, KOHAKU?

EH?

THIS OPPONENT OF MINE, INU-YASHA...
...IS HE HAND-SOME?

I WONDER WHAT COLOR HIS BLOOD IS?

SCROLL EIGHT
THE BAND OF SEVEN

INU-
YASHA,
OVER
THERE...

NO...
IS IT A
WAR?
KLOP
KLOP

EVEN
SO...IT'S
IMPRESSIVE.
I'D SAY THEY'RE
GOING...
TO
EXTERMINATE
SOMETHING.

...THAT THE GHOSTS OF THE *SEVEN* ARE HAUNTING US?

DO YOU SUPPOSE IT'S TRUE...

THE SEPULCHER HAS BEEN OPENED...
...THAT HOLDS THE GHOSTS OF THE BAND OF SEVEN.
AND THEY ARE...?

IT'S A TALE FROM DECADES PAST.
THEY CAME HERE FROM A LAND FAR TO THE EAST...

A BAND OF SEVEN SOLDIERS-FOR-HIRE, VASSALS TO NO LORD...
THEY DRIFTED FROM BATTLE TO BATTLE, FIGHTING FOR ANY WHO WOULD PAY THEM.

THEY WERE POWERFUL BEYOND WORDS.
IT WAS SAID THAT THE SEVEN DID THE WORK OF 100 SOLDIERS.

SOME HAVE SAID THAT THEY WERE JUST A GANG OF THUGS WHO LOVED TO KILL FROM THE DEPTHS OF THEIR SOULS.
...
OH MY...
AND THEIR METHODS WERE BRUTAL BEYOND WORDS.
THOSE WHO MET THE SEVEN WERE HACKED TO BITS, BURNED BEYOND RECOGNITION.
NOT EVEN WOMEN AND CHILDREN SPARED.
BECAUSE OF THEIR POWER AND CRUELTY...
...THE LOCAL LORDS WHO HAD COME TO FEAR THEM SET OUT TO SUPPRESS THEM. UNFORTUNATELY...

...THAT PROVED TO BE VERY DIFFICULT.
I CAN IMAGINE.

THE BAND OF SEVEN ROUTED THEIR PURSUERS AND FLED INTO THE MOUNTAINS-
-BUT FINALLY THEY WERE CAPTURED-
-COMPLETELY OUTNUMBERED- IN A DESERTED VILLAGE NORTH OF HERE.

THEY WERE ALL BEHEADED AND BURIED.
BUT THE PEOPLE FEARED THAT EVEN DEATH WOULD NOT DEFEAT THEM.
SO THEY ERECTED A MONUMENT TO APPEASE THEIR ANGRY SOULS.

AND THAT IS THE BURIAL MOUND OF THE SEVEN.
I SEE...

UM...
YOU SAID SOMETHING ABOUT THESE GHOSTS HAUNTING YOU...?

GHOSTS, EH?

WHAT DO YOU THINK, LORD MONK?

WE'VE ALREADY SEEN HOW MANY PETTY DEMONS HAVE CRAWLED OUT OF THE GROUND NOW THAT NARAKU'S AURA HAS VANISHED...

I DON'T CARE IF THEY'RE GHOSTS OR DEMONS.

IF WE BUMP INTO 'EM, WE'LL JUST CUT 'EM DOWN.
WE'RE HEADED IN THAT DIRECTION ANYWAY.

D-D-D-D-DM
D-DM
D-DM
D-DM
D-DM

WEAVE~

HOY! YOU THERE!
CLEAR THE ROAD!

EH?

JERK
PRRRRR

DID YOU JUST SAY SOMETHING?

AH. THEN I TAKE IT...
...THAT YOU HAVE NO IDEA WHAT THE GHOSTS LOOK LIKE.

HYOON

VSH
WHAT...?

YOU SEE...
I'M ONE
OF THEM.

SUR-
ROUND
HIM!
Y-YOU?!

SHHM

SIGH
WHAT MEMORIES THIS BRINGS BACK...

HYUU

IMPOSSIBLE!
HOW CAN SWING YOUR BLADE FROM SO FAR-

OH...
VISH

WHAT...

WHAT STRANGE MAGIC IS THIS...?!

TEE HEE HEE...
NO MAGIC AT ALL.

NOT NOW. NOT BEFORE.
HYUUU

THE SCENT OF BLOOD?!
YEAH-AND NOT JUST A FEW PEOPLE, EITHER!
AND NOT JUST BLOOD...BUT ANOTHER SMELL...
...FAINT, BUT... IT'S THERE...!
THE SMELL-
OF GRAVE SOIL!!

YOU DON'T MEAN-
THEY WERE ALL SLAUGHTERED BY HIM?
THESE ARE THE PEOPLE WHO RODE THROUGH THE VILLAGE EARLIER...

...INU-YASHA?!
DON'T TELL ME! ARE YOU REALLY...
EH?

HOW DO YOU KNOW ABOUT ME?!
WHAT?!
!

MMM.
YOU **ARE** PRETTY!!

UH...?

THOSE EARS ARE ADORABLE!
I THINK I'LL TAKE THEM...

WHAT AM I UP AGAINST ***NOW?!***

SCROLL NINE
JYAKOTSU

ANSWER!
JUST WHO AND WHAT ARE YOU?!

YOU STINK OF CORPSES... AND GRAVE SOIL!
YOU DON'T SMELL LIKE A LIVING MAN!

SIGH.

YEAH.
PERHAPS HE'S...

ABOUT SOME EVIL GHOSTS WHO ESCAPED FROM THEIR GRAVES.
THE LOCALS ARE TRADING RUMORS, YOU KNOW.

A BAND OF SEVEN KILLERS...
MERCENARIES WHO WERE CHASED DOWN BY THE LAW AND BEHEADED!
ARE YOU ONE OF THE BAND OF SEVEN?!

...
AN-SWER ME.
INU-YASHA IS SIMPLY LOVELY, BUT...
...YOU'RE AN AWFULLY SEXY MONK.
I WANT TO MAKE YOU SCREAM.

RRG...

MIND IF I USE THE WIND TUNNEL?
PLEASE DO.
NO... WAIT...
KLATTER

THE SHIKON SHARD...

WHO IMPLANTED IT IN YOU?!

HEE HEE HEE...

YOU'RE BEAUTIFUL WHEN YOU'RE ANGRY.

GLEEM

ZH!

SHUT UP, YOU FREAK!

I'LL MAKE YOU SPILL EVERYTHING YOU KNOW!!

...IF IT'S AS INTERESTING AS MINE!
HSH
!?

ZIP
IT'S A TRICK BLADE!
STEP BACK!

THE WAY THOSE SOLDIERS WERE SLAUGHTERED...
I THOUGHT IT WAS STRANGE...

CLINK
TEE HEE.

ALL KILLED AT ONCE-
WITHOUT EVEN A CHANCE TO CROSS BLADES WITH HIM!

I THOUGHT IT WAS JUST A LONG SWITCHBLADE...
...BUT IT'S ACTUALLY...

WSH

ZSH
!
EH...?
INU-YASHA!

A BENDABLE BLADE?!

WELL, WHAT DO YOU THINK?
IN THE BAND OF SEVEN THEY NAMED ME AFTER MY BLADE...

JYAKOTSU... THE "SNAKE BONE"!
KSSH

YOU EVIL LITTLE...

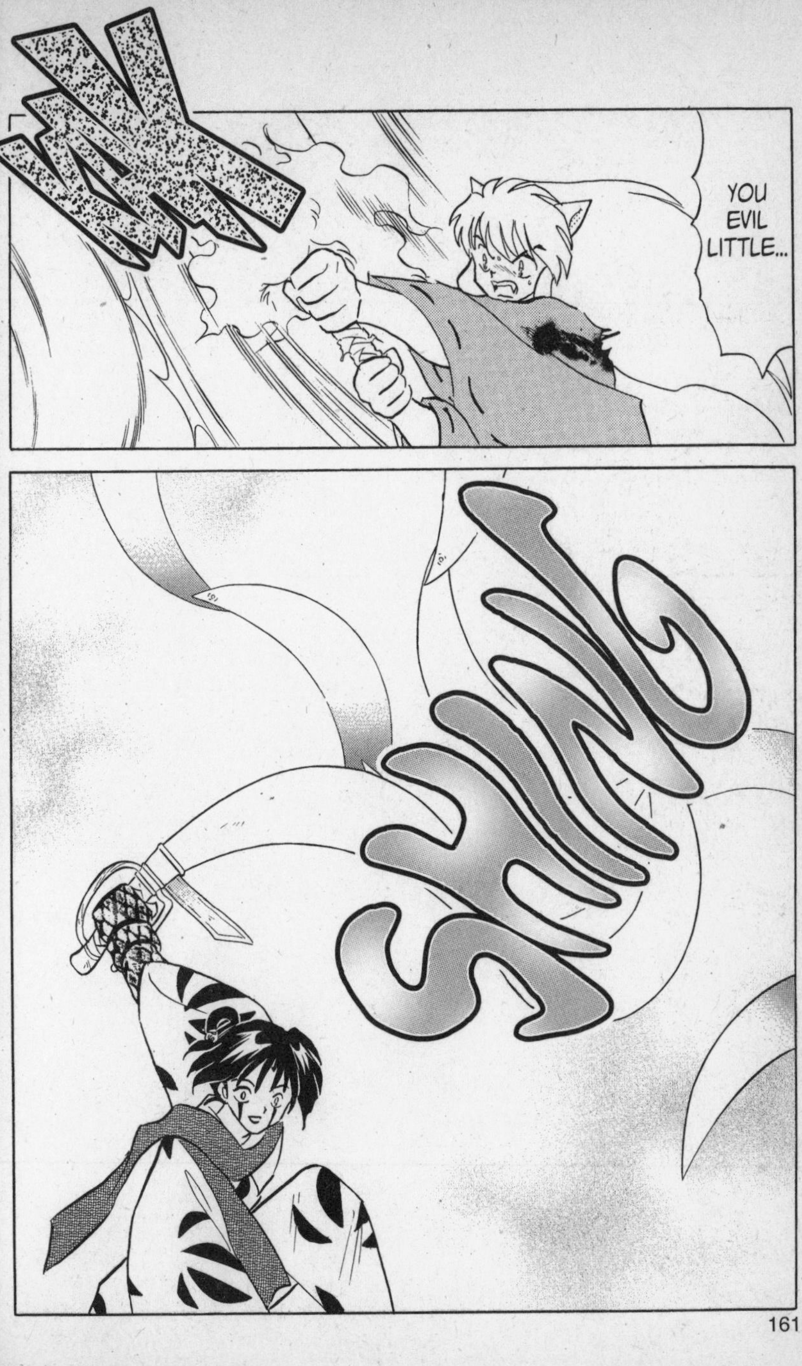

SHING

NGH!

HEH.

!
VSH
GRUUU---
THUK

IT REALLY IS LIKE A SNAKE!
EVEN IF HE DE-FLECTS IT... IT BOUNCES BACK!

SHHH...
RUN AROUND SOME MORE!

SHAA
!

SHUUU
DG DG DG DG

TEE HEE.
CHK

I CAN'T TELL WHERE HIS BLADE IS GONNA COME FROM!
DAMN IT...

HSH
I WANT TO KEEP SEEING IT.

IT MAKES ME SHIVER.
I LIKE THAT EXPRES-SION ON YOUR FACE.

BOOMERANG BONE!

VNNNN
!

TWING

UGH!!

WHACK
GYAA!
OH!

!

SANGO!
I-I'M ALL RIGHT... IT ONLY GRAZED ME...

CHK

STAY OUT OF THIS... *WOMAN!*
DON'T YOU DARE INTERFERE WITH MY FUN!!

YOU'RE MAKING ME SICK!

VVVV
SO HEART-LESS.
SIIIIGH-
STING

ANSWER ME NOW!!
SHUT UP!! WHO GAVE YOU THAT SHIKON SHARD?!

GEH-HEH-HEH.... THEY'RE GOING AT IT...
THAT JYAKOTSU! HE HASN'T CHANGED A BIT!
HSSS...
HYOOO---

SCROLL TEN

POISON SMOKE

JYAKOTSU! THE ONE WHO IMPLANTED THE SHARD IN YOU-

IT WAS NARAKU, WASN'T IT?!

IF YOU'RE LYING TO ME-
HSHH
?!

SSHHH
!
SMOKE...?!

SHH
!
SSS...
BLUK BLUK

THAT'S... POISON SMOKE!!
THEY'RE... MELTING...?!

WHA...?
INU-YASHA...
YOU'D BETTER RUN TOO!
SKIP

INTER-FERING AGAIN!
TSK! THAT NASTY MUKOTSU!

!
SSSS

TSH
WAIT, YOU!

WE'LL MEET AGAIN... HANDSOME.
SSSSSS...
BLUK BLUK

DAMN IT!
BM

UGH...

PLEASE WAIT, LORD SESSHŌMARU!
SHF SHF

I SMELL IT...
DM...
IT'S HIM...
NARAKU'S UNDERLING...
THE CHILD.

LORD JYAKEN!
WHAT'S LORD SESSHŌ-MARU LOOKING FOR?
NARAKU, OF COURSE!

WHEN YOU WERE KIDNAPPED, RIN...
...OUR LORD GREW VERY ANGRY!

OVER ME?!
GLINT
DON'T LET IT GO TO YOUR HEAD.

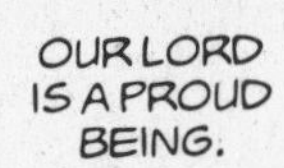

OUR LORD IS A PROUD BEING.
HE MAY APPEAR SERENE AND COM-POSED...
...BUT WHEN SOMEONE PULLS A TRICK LIKE THAT ON HIM, HE IS MOST DISPLEASED.

...

MUST WATCH THIS MOUTH...
ARE YOU ALL RIGHT?
THROB

HSH

WILL YOU GO AFTER HIM, INU-YASHA?
THAT JYAKOTSU COULDN'T HAVE GOTTEN FAR YET.
I'M... ALL RIGHT.
DOES IT HURT, SANGO?

YOU'RE RIGHT. SINCE SANGO'S INJURED...
...BUT INU-YASHA...
INU-YASHA...
YOU ALL WAIT HERE.
DAMN RIGHT! WE STILL HAVEN'T ANY CLUES OUT OF HIM!

WHAT DO YOU THINK OF THAT POISON SMOKE?
IT SEEMED AS IF JYAKOTSU KNEW SOME-THING ABOUT IT...

YEAH...
IT MIGHT'VE BEEN FROM ANOTHER ONE OF THE BAND OF SEVEN.

THEN YOU THINK THERE ARE LEAST TWO...?

MIROKU, YOU STAY HERE AND PROTECT KAGOME AND SANGO.
OF COURSE.

HSSH

GEH-HEH HEH! THEY'VE DIVIDED INTO TWO GROUPS, EH?
BZZ...
I COULDN'T ASK FOR MORE!

SHK

YO, JYAKOTSU.

LONG TIME NO SEE.

LITTLE SNOT.

MOOSH...

SO, WHAT ARE YOU GOING TO DO, JYAKOTSU?

I'M HEADING OUT TO WHERE THE WOMEN ARE.

MM?

INU-YASHA'S COMING AFTER ME ALONE?!
PING
OH!!

PLUS...THAT WOMAN KAGOME HAS SHIKON SHARDS!
GRIND GRIND
GEH-HEH HEH HEH... THE OTHERS ARE JUST A FEW HUMANS AND A JUVENILE FOX DEMON.

YOU'RE LETTING ME HAVE THE SHARDS?
ARE YOU SURE?
YEAH?
I'LL LEAVE THEM TO YOU.
SCRITCH SCRITCH

FINE. WHO NEEDS HIM?
GRIND GRIND
ALL I WANT IS INU-YASHA.
GO AHEAD.

LET'S GO HOME BEFORE THE SUN SETS, EH?
YEAH... ESPECIALLY WITH ALL THOSE STORIES ABOUT GHOSTS RUNNING WILD...

...SSS

POP

HYURURURU
SHUUUU
EH?

GREAT!
KAGOME, A WELL.
CHIRIRIN
LET'S ASK IF WE CAN HAVE SOME WATER...

OH NO!
KRIK
SOME-ONE'S COL-LAPSED!

SSS...

KAGOME... LET'S GET OUT OF HERE NOW.

SHE'S DEAD?!

ARE YOU ALL RIGHT?!
MA'AM?

...SSS

...SHH

!

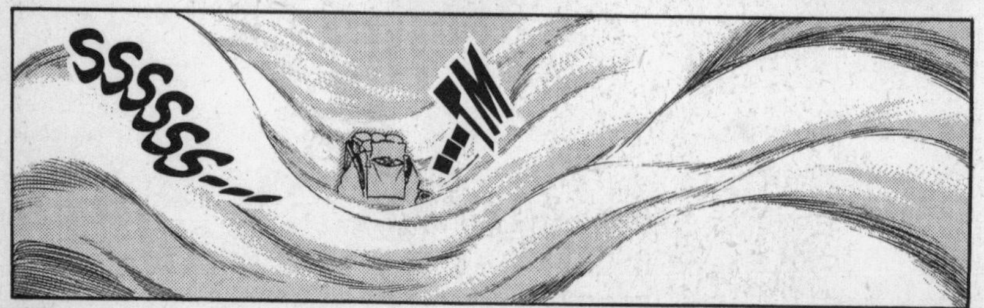

GEH-HEH-HEH-HEH... YOU CAN NEVER ESCAPE...
TWIIII
...FROM THE POISON OF LORD MUKOTSU!
--SSSSS

NO WAY!
SHIPPO...
R...RUN...

KAGO-
ME?!
NGK...

THE LITTLE LASS WHO HAS THE SHIKON SHARDS.
...TM
GEH-HEH-HEH-HEH... SO YOU'RE THE ONE!

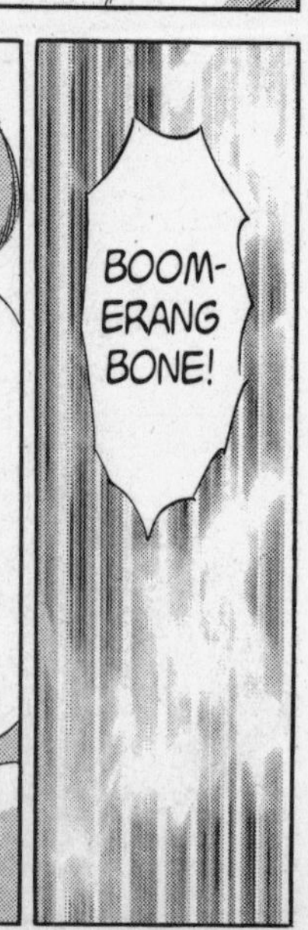
BOOM-
ERANG
BONE!

ONLY PARALYZES YOU...BUT YOU WON'T PASS OUT UNTIL THE VERY END.
I LIKE TO PLAY WITH MY WOMEN... UNTIL THE VERY END.
...TM

YOU SEE, THIS POISON...
DON'T WORRY... I WON'T KILL YOU RIGHT AWAY.
...TM

WHOA!
KRAK

FAP
HSS

THIS POISON DOESN'T WORK AGAINST DEMONS!
I CAN STILL MOVE... THAT MEANS...

DON'T COME CLOSER... THE POISON WILL KILL YOU...

SANGO... MIROKU...

I'LL GO GET INU-YASHA!
VSH
HANG IN THERE, KAGOME!

SSS...

NOW... WHICH POISON SHOULD I TREAT YOU TO...?

GEH-HEH HEH HEH! THIS IS STARTING TO BE FUN!

TO BE CONTINUED...

About Rumiko Takahashi

Born in 1957 in Niigata, Japan, Rumiko Takahashi attended women's college in Tokyo, where she began studying comics with Kazuo Koike, author of *Crying Freeman*. She later became an assistant to horror-manga artist Kazuo Umezu (*Orochi*). In 1978, she won a prize in Shogakukan's annual "New Comic Artist Contest," and in that same year her boy-meets-alien comedy series *Urusei Yatsura* began appearing in the weekly manga magazine *Shônen Sunday*. This phenomenally successful series ran for nine years and sold over 22 million copies. Takahashi's later *Ranma 1/2* series enjoyed even greater popularity.

Takahashi is considered by many to be one of the world's most popular manga artists. With the publication of Volume 34 of her *Ranma 1/2* series in Japan, Takahashi's total sales passed *one hundred million* copies of her compiled works.

Takahashi's serial titles include *Urusei Yatsura*, *Ranma 1/2*, *One-Pound Gospel*, *Maison Ikkoku* and *InuYasha*. Additionally, Takahashi has drawn many short stories which have been published in America under the title "Rumic Theater," and several installments of a saga known as her "Mermaid" series. Most of Takahashi's major stories have also been animated and are widely available in translation worldwide. *InuYasha* is her most recent serial story, first published in *Shônen Sunday* in 1996.

All New ACTION Graphic Novels!

VIZ media

www.viz.com

store.viz.com:

Bastard!!, Vol. 10
Case Closed, Vol. 9
Cheeky Angel, Vol. 10
Fullmetal Alchemist, Vol. 5
Inuyasha, Vol. 24 *
MÄR, Vol. 5
Midori Days, Vol. 3
Project Arms, Vol. 11 *
Video Girl Ai: Len's Story, Vol. 14 *

** Also available on DVD from VIZ*

LOVE MANGA? LET US KNOW!

☐ Please do NOT send me information about VIZ Media products, news and events, special offers, or other information.

☐ Please do NOT send me information from VIZ Media's trusted business partners.

Name: ______________________________

Address: ______________________________

City: ______________ **State:** ________ **Zip:** ____________

E-mail: ______________________________

☐ **Male** ☐ **Female** **Date of Birth** (mm/dd/yyyy): ____/____/______ (**Under 13? Parental consent required**)

What race/ethnicity do you consider yourself? (check all that apply)

☐ White/Caucasian ☐ Black/African American ☐ Hispanic/Latino

☐ Asian/Pacific Islander ☐ Native American/Alaskan Native ☐ Other: ____________

What VIZ Media title(s) did you purchase? (indicate title(s) purchased) ______________________________

____

What other VIZ Media titles do you own? ______________________________

____

Reason for purchase: (check all that apply)

☐ Special offer ☐ Favorite title / author / artist / genre

☐ Gift ☐ Recommendation ☐ Collection

☐ Read excerpt in VIZ Media manga sampler ☐ Other ____________

Where did you make your purchase? (please check one)

☐ Comic store ☐ Bookstore ☐ Grocery Store

☐ Convention ☐ Newsstand ☐ Video Game Store

☐ Online (site: ______________) ☐ Other ____________

How many manga titles have you purchased in the last year? How many were VIZ Media titles?
(please check one from each column)

MANGA	VIZ Media
☐ None	☐ None
☐ 1 – 4	☐ 1 – 4
☐ 5 – 10	☐ 5 – 10
☐ 11+	☐ 11+

How much influence do special promotions and gifts-with-purchase have on the titles you buy?
(please circle, with 5 being great influence and 1 being none)

1 2 3 4 5

Do you purchase every volume of your favorite series?

☐ Yes! Gotta have 'em as my own ☐ No. Please explain: ______________

What kind of manga storylines do you most enjoy? **(check all that apply)**

☐ Action / Adventure	☐ Science Fiction	☐ Horror
☐ Comedy	☐ Romance (shojo)	☐ Fantasy (shojo)
☐ Fighting	☐ Sports	☐ Historical
☐ Artistic / Alternative	☐ Other ______________	

If you watch the anime or play a video or TCG game from a series, how likely are you to buy the manga? **(please circle, with 5 being very likely and 1 being unlikely)**

1 2 3 4 5

If unlikely, please explain: ______________

Who are your favorite authors / artists? ______________

____

What titles would like you translated and sold in English? ______________

____

THANK YOU! Please send the completed form to:

NJW Research
42 Catharine Street
Poughkeepsie, NY 12601

Your privacy is very important to us. All information provided will be used for internal purposes only and will not be sold or otherwise divulged.